Change Your Sauce, Change Your Life

~ Easy Plant Based Sauces
to Blend, Whisk, and Shake ~
from Positively Vegan

By Kim Miles
PositivelyVegan.Blogspot.com
Studio13Press

For Rick, with love and gratitude
xoxo

Copyright 2016 Kim Miles
All rights reserved.
ISBN-13: 978-1523260232
ISBN-10: 1523260238

Contents

The Sauces

Salad Dressings

Simple Meals to Put Under Your Sauces

Introduction

Eating well, and also eating *good*, as in really tasty, made-with-love food, are high priorities in my world. I don't, however, often feel like making a big deal over a meal, or a big mess in the kitchen. When I began cooking vegan fare for my husband, Rick, and myself, we were traveling in an RV with a *very* limited kitchen. Later, back at home, I continued in our small, "vintage 1975" Taos, NM kitchen. Now I make the most of our micro "Euro Style" kitchen in our 571 square foot studio apartment in Portland, Oregon. None of it has ever been ideal.

I suspect that most of us have never had the luxury of an upgraded, modern home kitchen, or a shiny commercial kitchen. Still, we need to eat, and we love good food. I've discovered though, that it's not the kitchen's job to inspire me. It's up to me to step up to the challenge of creating food magic in whatever space I have.

Most of us, vegan or not, rely on only a handful of favorite dishes that we're comfortable making, and we tend to eat those over and over again. There's nothing wrong with that, except that it can get kind of boring.

We also have several favorite go-to meals, but we don't get tired of what we eat. My solution is sauce! In my opinion, sauce makes the meal. And by changing up the sauce, you can easily transform your favorite meals into new and exciting adventures. Take, for instance, a humble burrito, filled with wonderful beans, greens, veggies, and vegan cheese. It's good, it's easy, and you know how to make it. Good enough, right?

Now imagine that same burrito on a favorite plate, smothered (as they say in New Mexico) in spicy Red or Green Chile, or Cheese Sauce, or Mole, or even Mushroom-Cashew Gravy! Suddenly you have five new meals to consider, and all you have to change is the sauce.

The same goes for stir-fries, pastas, salads, and grain bowls. It's really that easy.

The recipes in this book offer variations and suggestions to spark your creativity. At the back of the book you'll find a few basic un-recipes for what to put under your sauces, in case you're really new to plant-based cooking. Experiment, make them your own, and use the *Cook's Notes* pages to keep track of what you do and what you like.

This little book is a reflection of how Rick and I actually eat, and how well we've learned to not just function, but to thrive in funky, inadequate kitchens. The book is small, even minimal, because I wanted it to be filled with only good basics that can be made almost anywhere. I have dozens of cookbooks that are padded with far more recipes than I'll ever use. The recipes in this book are time tested over five years of happy plant-based eating. These are recipes we go back to over and over again, and I hope you will too.

Change your sauce, change your life. Yes, really. You'll see.

Equipment

While the recipes in this book are all simple to make, sauces are generally smooth, and so need to be blended in some way. The following represent a range of blending options, from the fanciest and most expensive to the most basic and affordable. Each recipe tells you what's best to use, as well as what will work if it's all you've got. Get the best equipment you can, and add to your collection over time.

Blender – Most of the recipes here are best made in a high-speed blender, like Vitamix or Blendtec. These make the smoothest sauces, as well as smoothies, soups, and other thicker things like hummus and even peanut butter. If you can, invest in one of these sooner, rather than later. You're going to want one eventually. A regular (less expensive) blender will do, but your sauces will not be as smooth, and it won't have the versatility or added super-powers of a really good high-speed blender. I've spent a lot of money on cheap blenders that didn't do a great job, and didn't last more than a year or two. If I'd bought the Vitamix I have now in the beginning, I think I'd have actually come out ahead.

NutriBullet – This is newer breed of blender that has the blades in a lid that screws onto the bottom of the mixing jar and seats on the base with the motor in it. The "Bullet" has a fair amount of power in short bursts and does a good job of blending and smoothing sauces. It's intended for smoothies, and does well with those. The downsides are, the capacity is rather small, it's messy to open to add more ingredients, and you can't blend hot liquids with it at all.

Food Processor – These are great for thick spreads and sauces, and not so great for thinner liquids, which tend to leak up through the center, where the blade is seated. They're also nice in the prep department if you get one with grater and slicer attachments. For a while I only had a food processor, and it was fine for everything I was making. When I wanted to add smoothies to the menu, I had to get a blender.

Immersion Blender – Also called stick blenders, these hand-held electric wands are plunged right into whatever you're mixing, even hot sauces or soups. The small but sharp blades do a good job of smoothing out lumpy gravies, chile sauces, and also soups. These will also mix smoothies or shakes in a tall glass. An immersion blender is not the best choice for sauces with nuts in them. It is, however, a really handy tool to have around.

Whisk & Jar – Low tech and elegant, a good wire whisk is sometimes all you need to whip together a simple sauce or salad dressing. A jar with a tight-fitting lid can shake up a simple sauce or salad dressing, and double as a serving and storage container.

Ingredients

Most of the ingredients in these recipes are regular things you probably already have on hand, or have at least heard of. A few might be "weird vegan ingredients" to you, but they're key to the rich, layered flavors of certain sauces, so don't be afraid to get to know them!

Raw Cashews – Cashews are the "wonder nut" of the vegan cooking world. They blend elegantly into the most creamy, smooth sauces imaginable, and I use a lot of them. Broken pieces are usually cheaper than whole cashews. Just be sure to buy them raw, rather than roasted and/or salted. To use raw cashews, soak them in cold water for 20 minutes or more. Drain and rinse them in a colander, and then follow the recipe's instructions.

Nutritional Yeast – Nicknamed "nooch," this yeast is not anything like baking yeast or brewer's yeast. It's a type of deactivated yeast that's grown on molasses. It has trace minerals and some B vitamins, and is sometimes fortified with B12. Don't depend on it for any of your real nutritional needs though. Love it for the nutty, cheesy flavor it adds to so many things, like cheese sauce! It's also delicious sprinkled on salad, soups, and popcorn, or anything you might use Parmesan cheese on.

Plant Based Milk – Unsweetened, unflavored, almond, soy, hemp, coconut, rice, and oat milks are all good choices in any of my recipes. Use what you have, and what you like. You can also easily make your own if you have a good blender.

Coconut Milk – I'm talking about the kind that generally comes in a can. It's thick and creamy and adds amazing richness to sauces and soups. Depending on how much fat you want in your finished dish, choose either regular or light varieties. The full fat kind does taste better, but the "lite" will do just fine.

Tofu – Tofu comes in several varieties and firmnesses, both refrigerated and on the shelf in the Asian section of some markets. I usually buy the one pound refrigerated blocks. Silken tofu is very smooth, soft, and delicate, making it perfect for sauces. Extra firm tofu is great for scrambles. Look for organic, non-GMO tofu. It's easy to find.

Ground Flax Seed – (Flax Meal) - When you add water to flax seeds, they form a gel that makes them particularly good for thickening sauces. They need to be ground up in order for your body to absorb the nutrients. Once they're ground, they will go rancid fairly quickly at room temperature. Buy whole flax seeds and grind them in a coffee grinder or small food processor, and store them in the refrigerator, where they'll keep for about six months.

Chia Seeds – This tiny "super food" seed has similar qualities to those of flax seeds. They do not need to be ground or refrigerated, however. They're pretty much interchangeable in my recipes calling for flax meal. They will be more visible in a finished sauce, even if it's been blended.

Tamari – This is my favorite type of soy sauce. It's usually wheat-free, but check the label if you want to be sure it's gluten free. I like to buy the low-sodium variety, so I have more control over how much salt goes into what I'm cooking. Tamari can round out and add depth to almost any savory dish, and can be used in place of salt. Don't reserve it only for Asian-style foods.

Kelp Granules – Often used as a salt substitute, these little green granules add a mild seafood-ish flavor to whatever you use them in.

Miso – or Miso Paste – Most often made from fermented soybeans, this flavorful paste adds a lovely depth to many sauces, and also makes a terrific soup. It's salty, so add it gradually when going beyond what a recipe calls for. Never boil miso, as it damages the healthy enzymes. When shopping, keep in mind that the darker the color, the more flavorful the miso will be. I tend to go for red or brown miso. If you avoid soy, look for miso made from chickpeas or adzuki beans.

Tahini – Sesame seeds are the main ingredient in tahini. You can make your own, or in a pinch, substitute an equal amount of toasted or raw sesame seeds in sauces requiring a blender.

Green Curry Paste – You can make your own curry paste, but there's no real need to. It's easy to find a variety of brands in Asian markets and online. The little jar found in most supermarkets is not the best. Just sayin'. Two that I like, and order on Amazon, are Mae Anong and Maesri. They keep almost forever in the refrigerator.

Chipotle Peppers in Adobo – Chipotle peppers are smoked jalapenos. If that wasn't already wonderful enough, you can buy them in tangy-sweet adobo sauce, which is exactly the right boost for certain dishes. They're easy to find in the Mexican Foods section of most markets.

Chipotle Powder – Smoked jalapeno peppers, ground into powder are a terrific seasoning no kitchen should be without. It's spicy though. Be careful!

Ginger Root – The fresh root tastes much different from the powdered spice. Buy it in the produce department of most markets and store it in the refrigerator. As you need it, scrape the thin skin away with the edge of a teaspoon before chopping or grating.

Umeboshi Plum Paste – This exotic condiment is made from Japanese pickled plums. It has a strong salty-sour taste that adds a great kick to certain dishes. It's a little pricey, and not absolutely necessary, but consider it when you feel like a fun food adventure.

Maple Syrup – Buy only 100% pure maple syrup. The less expensive B grade is good. It can be used in place of agave syrup in my recipes.

Agave Syrup – This thick liquid sweetener is a good substitute for maple syrup, or for when you want a milder, less distinguishable flavor.

Carob Powder – I call for this in only one recipe, the New Mexican Mole, but it's an essential ingredient. Make sure it's unsweetened, and keep it around for baking, hot drinks, chia seed pudding, and the Mole Sauce you'll want to make over and over again.

Oils – My two favorite oils are good olive oil for low-heat cooking and salad dressings, and coconut oil for high-heat cooking. Refined coconut oil is more neutral in flavor and smell, while unrefined has a wonderful coconut aroma.

The Sauces - Here we go!

My Favorite Cheese Sauce
makes about 3 cups
blender or food processor

There are lots of vegan cheese sauce recipes out there, and I've been tinkering with this one for years. I like it better than any I've tried so far. It's creamy and rich, and wonderful on mac n' cheese, scrambles, steamed veggies, burritos, and even mashed potatoes. You can also make it into a thick spread by reducing the water and salt by half. A Vitamix or food processor can handle the extra thickness.

Ingredients
1/2 cup raw cashews, soaked 20 minutes or more
1/2 cup cooked, rinsed garbanzo beans
1/2 cup nutritional yeast
1/2 - 1 tsp salt (to taste)
1/2 tsp paprika
1/2 tsp sweet smoked paprika
1/2 tsp garlic powder
1 tsp mustard powder
1/4 cup raw or toasted sesame seeds
1 T miso
1 T tamari
2 T white or apple cider vinegar
2 T olive oil (optional)
1 cup water

Instructions
Place all ingredients in a blender. Blend at highest speed until smooth.
Pour the sauce into a pan and heat it over low heat on the stove.
(cont.)

Or, if you have a Vitamix or similar blender, use boiling water and blend for one to two minutes. The friction in a high-speed blender actually heats the sauce. One less pan to wash! (Do *not* try this with a NutriBullet – only with high-speed blenders designed to be used with hot liquids.)

Variations
Add 1-2 tablespoons chili powder and 1 teaspoon cumin for a spicy southwest version.
Add 1-2 teaspoons Herbes de Provence, dried basil, or fresh herbs from your garden.

Cook's Notes:

Cook's Notes:

Queso for Dipping and Nachos
makes about 2 cups
blender or food processor

Queso (KAY-so) means "cheese" in Spanish. It also refers to a thick, spicy dipping sauce that's perfect with warmed tortilla chips, or poured over nachos or burritos. For dipping, serve it in a small bowl or mini electric crock-pot. This is best warm, so it's better to refill a small bowl than to let a larger amount get cold.

Ingredients
1 cup raw cashews, soaked 20 minutes or more
1/4 cup nutritional yeast
1/4 cup chipotle peppers in adobo
2 T arrowroot
1/2 tsp garlic powder
1/2 tsp salt (or to taste)
2 tsp miso
1 T Dijon mustard
1 cup water

Optional Stir-ins:
1 small (4 oz) can diced green chiles
1/4 cup corn kernels
1/4 cup chopped tomatoes
1/4 cup chopped black olives

Instructions
Place all ingredients except Stir-ins in a blender or food processor, and blend about one minute or until smooth.
Pour the Queso into a saucepan, toss in desired Stir-ins, and warm over low heat, stirring often. Add a little more water if it gets too thick.

Cook's Notes:

Creamy Alfredo Sauce
makes about 4 cups
blender or food processor

I used to make a total fat-bomb Alfredo sauce out of cream cheese, butter, and heavy cream. This version is plenty rich and decadent, and a whole lot healthier. Serve it over pasta, on pizza, on tofu scrambles with spinach, or over steamed vegetables with rice or quinoa. It's pretty amazing.

Ingredients
1 cup raw cashews, soaked in water for 20 minutes or more
1 lb package silken tofu
3 cloves garlic
1/2 cup nutritional yeast
1/2 tsp onion powder
1/2 - 1 tsp salt (to taste)
1/4 tsp white pepper (or black)
2 tsp dry basil
1 tsp dry oregano
1/2 cup white wine
1 cup water (or plant based milk to make it extra rich)

Instructions
Place all ingredients in a blender or food processor, and blend on high speed until smooth and creamy. Warm over low heat in a saucepan.

Variation
If you avoid soy, or want a lower fat sauce, substitute about 2 1/2 cups of steamed cauliflower for the tofu. It's a little more work, but it tastes incredible.

Cook's Notes:

Cashew Wine & Cheese Sauce
makes about 2 1/2 cups
blender or food processor

This made-for-grownups version of cheese sauce gets all fancypants with the addition of white wine and truffle salt. Try serving it with pasta, over burritos filled with asparagus, cannellini beans, and sun-dried tomatoes, or thicken it with a tablespoon of arrowroot and dip bread in it, fondue style.

Ingredients
1 cup raw cashews, soaked 20 minutes or more
1/4 cup nutritional yeast
1 tsp garlic powder
1/2 tsp truffle salt (or regular salt)
1/2 tsp paprika
2 T olive oil
1/2 cup dry white wine
1/2 tsp apple cider vinegar
1 rounded tsp Dijon mustard
1/2 cup water or plant based milk

Instructions
Place all ingredients in a blender or food processor, and blend on high speed until smooth, about one minute. Warm slowly in a saucepan stirring often.

Cook's Notes:

Red Chile
makes about 4 cups
blender, immersion blender, or un-blended

The official state question of New Mexico, where I lived for 13 years, is, "Red or Green?" Really. Choose one or the other, or ask for "Christmas," which is both. The heat of this sauce will depend on the chile powders you use. When in doubt, use only mild chile powder and put a bottle of hot sauce on the table for the heat lovers. It's also a nice touch to offer a bottle of homemade *Crema* (page 27) to help cool things down and add balance to your spicy dishes.

Ingredients
2 T coconut oil
1 yellow onion, finely chopped
1 T garlic, chopped
3 T mild chile powder
1 tsp hot chile powder
2 tsp cumin powder
1/2 tsp cinnamon
1 (32 oz) carton vegetable broth
1/4 cup nutritional yeast
2 T ground flaxseed (or chia seeds)
2 T arrowroot
2 T maple syrup (or agave)
1 cup frozen corn (optional)
1 tsp salt (or to taste)

(cont.)

Instructions

Sauté the onion in oil until soft. Add the garlic and spices, and cook for 1-2 minutes. Cooking the spices before adding liquid makes a huge difference in the flavor. Don't skip this step! Add the broth, nutritional yeast, maple syrup, flax seed, arrowroot, and corn. Bring to a near-boil, then reduce the heat to low and cook for 10-15 minutes. It will thicken as it cooks. This sauce is great un-blended, but to make it smoother, an immersion blender is easiest.

Cook's Notes:

Green Chile

makes about 6 cups
blender, immersion blender, or un-blended

Use Green Chile interchangeably with Red Chile (see previous) on burritos, enchiladas, and scrambles, or turn it into a simple, hearty stew by adding potatoes, carrots, zucchini, red bell peppers, beans, chopped kale, corn, and maybe some cooked hominy.

Ingredients
1 onion, chopped
oil for sautéing (optional)
2-3 cloves garlic, chopped
1/4 cup flour (wheat or gluten free), mixed with 1 cup water
4 cups vegetable broth
2 cups chopped Hatch green chiles
1 tsp cumin
1 tsp dry oregano
salt to taste

Instructions
Fry the onion and garlic in a little water (or oil), over medium heat, for about 3 minutes.
Add the flour/water mixture, and cook for 3 minutes, stirring constantly.
Add the broth, chiles, cumin, and oregano.
Bring to a boil, then reduce heat to low and simmer for 30 minutes, stirring often.
Blend with an immersion blender, or leave the sauce chunky if you prefer.
Add salt to taste.

Cook's Notes:

New Mexican Mole
makes about 3 1/2 cups
blender

Mole (MO-lay) is a complex, exotic sauce found in good
Mexican restaurants. The idea of attempting to make it at home
intimidates many cooks, but this easy recipe is something you
can enjoy often. Use mole on enchiladas, over fried, baked, or
grilled tofu or tempeh, on steamed or stir-fried vegetables, on
scrambles and burritos, and even as a salad dressing!

Ingredients
1/2 cup raw cashews
1 cup vegetable broth
3/4 cup carob powder
2 tsp garlic powder
1 tsp onion powder
1 T cumin
1 1/2 tsp chipotle powder
2 tsp chili powder
1/2 tsp cinnamon
1 1/2 tsp salt (or to taste)
3 T agave syrup (or maple syrup)
1/4 cup olive oil
juice of 1 lime (about 2 T)
1 can (14.5 oz) diced tomatoes

Instructions
Place the cashews and broth in your blender first, but don't
blend them just yet. The broth will soak the cashews for a few
minutes while you add everything else.
Add all other ingredients to the blender, in the order given. The
tomatoes go on top to keep all the powders from "poofing" out
of the blender. Blend until very smooth.
Pour as much of the sauce as possible into a saucepan.

(cont.)

Add 1/2 cup water to the blender, put the lid on, and shake it up to loosen all the last bits of sauce. Stir the water/sauce into the rest of the sauce, and you won't waste a bit.

Warm over medium-low heat, stirring often, or leave it cold if using in a baked dish or as a salad dressing.

Cook's Notes:

Cashew Sour Cream
makes about 1 1/2 cups
blender or food processor

This sour cream is so good on soups, tacos, burritos, and salads, and as a base for a dip. Stir in a packet of vegan onion soup mix and grab a bag of potato chips!

Ingredients
1 cup raw cashews, soaked 20 minutes
juice of 1 lemon (about 3 T)
1/2 tsp salt
1/2 cup water or unsweetened plant-based milk

Instructions
Drain and rinse the cashews, and place all ingredients in a blender or food processor. Blend on high speed until smooth. Add a little water if needed to get the desired consistency. The sour cream will thicken when chilled.
~~~

Crema
makes about 1 cup
blender

Mexican Crema is less thick and less sour than sour cream. It's nice to serve alongside spicy dishes as a drizzle to relieve some of the heat.

Ingredients
½ cup raw cashews, soaked at least 20 minutes
juice of 1 lime (about 2 T)
¼ tsp salt
1 T maple syrup
¼ cup water

(cont.)

Instructions

Place all ingredients in a blender, and blend at highest speed for about 1 minute, or until smooth. Store in a plastic squeeze bottle in the refrigerator.

Cook's Notes:

Three Ingredient Marinade and Stir-Fry Sauce
makes about 1/2 cup
whisk

This is the simplest sauce ever, and you only need a whisk to mix it up. Marinate sliced tofu (1 block, 12 slices) in this sauce for an hour or more, then bake it (along with the marinade) in an oiled pan, in a 350° oven for one hour, turning it half way through the cooking time. Or pour the sauce over a veggie stir-fry just before serving. If you want it thicker, add one tablespoon of arrowroot mixed with a little bit of water to the pan and stir. The arrowroot thickens as it heats.

Ingredients
1/4 cup tamari
1/4 cup maple syrup
1/2 tsp smoked paprika

Instructions
Pour tamari and maple syrup into a glass measuring cup. Add the paprika and stir with a small wire whisk.

Cook's Notes:

Peanut Sauce
makes about 3 cups
whisk, blender, food processor, immersion blender

Peanut sauce is one of those creamy wonders that tastes good on just about anything. Use whole coconut milk for extra richness, or low fat for a somewhat lighter sauce. Serve this over steamed or sautéed vegetables with rice or noodles, or use it as a dressing on a chilled kale-and-or-noodle salad.

Ingredients
1 cup peanut butter (or other nut butter)
1 (14 oz) can coconut milk (regular or lite)
juice of 1 lime (about 2 T)
1 T tamari
2 tsp miso
1 tsp Sriracha sauce
2 tsp maple syrup (or agave)
1 - 2 T fresh ginger root, grated

Instructions
Gently whisk everything together in a saucepan over low heat. For extra smooth sauce, mix everything in a blender and then transfer to the pan for warming. Adjust seasonings and add a little water if it gets too thick.

Cook's Notes:

Buddha Belly Sauce
makes about 2 1/2 cups
whisk

This is similar to peanut sauce, but the addition of tahini and curry paste make it even more interesting. Use this sauce anywhere you'd use peanut sauce, or pour it over a Buddha Bowl (cooked rice or other grain, topped with any steamed, roasted, or stir-fried vegetables you like. Add tofu, tempeh, or lentils for extra protein.

Ingredients
1/2 cup peanut butter (or other nut butter)
1/4 cup tahini
2 T red or green curry paste
2 T miso
1 T lime juice
1 T maple syrup
1 T tamari
1 (14 oz) can coconut milk (regular or lite)

Instructions
Place all ingredients except coconut milk in a saucepan. Gradually add the coconut milk, whisking as you go. Heat over low heat until the sauce is steamy but not boiling.

Cook's Notes:

Thai Green Curry Sauce
makes about 4 cups
spoon or whisk

This recipe comes straight from the Reethi Beach Resort in the Maldives, where my son and daughter-in-law enjoyed "the best green curry of their lives." I was surprised (and a little relieved) that the curry paste was not house-made, which goes to show we can make vacation-good food at home without having to go to too much trouble.
I haven't been able to find the curry paste they use, which comes from Dubai, but there are two really good brands you can order on Amazon. Mae Anong Green Curry Paste is my favorite, and Maesri is a close runner-up. Both are thick, fragrant, and ever so much more flavorful than the usual grocery store brand. They're spicy too, so be careful if that matters.

This sauce is amazing with any kind of rice or noodle dish. To make a meal like those served at the resort, reduce the heat and add any vegetables, tofu, or other additions you like. Simmer, stirring often, until vegetables are cooked. Stir in the chopped cilantro and lemon juice at the last minute. Serve over rice.

Ingredients
1 T coconut oil
1 yellow onion, chopped
2 large garlic cloves, chopped
2 T Thai Green Curry Paste
1 can regular coconut milk
1 can lite coconut milk
1 tsp fresh lemon juice
2 T fresh cilantro, chopped, plus a little more for garnish

(cont.)

Instructions

Heat the oil in a large saucepan. Add the onion and garlic, and stir-fry for 2-3 minutes. Add the curry paste and coconut milk, and let it bubble for 2 minutes. Add lemon and cilantro just before serving.

Cook's Notes:

Hoisin Sauce
makes about 1 cup
whisk or spoon

This sauce is often served along with Mu Shu Vegetables
stuffed inside little Mandarin Pancakes. Stir-fry any vegetables
you like with garlic, fresh ginger, and tamari. For the pancakes,
use your favorite batter, but make it less sweet than you would
for breakfast. Thin it down so the cakes are more like crepes,
and make them small, about 4 inches across. Fill the pancakes
with the veggies, add some Hoisin Sauce, and call it dinner.
Keep some on hand to use as a nice condiment alongside any
Asian-style dish. Marinate tofu, tempeh, or eggplant in it for
baking. Or thin it down with a little water and stir it into
cooked noodles or veggies.

2 T peanut butter
2 T tahini
1/4 cup tamari
1 T molasses
1 T maple syrup
1 T apple cider vinegar
1/2 tsp garlic powder
1/2 tsp Sriracha sauce

Instructions
Whisk all ingredients together and store in a jar in the
refrigerator. The sauce will thicken a little when it's chilled.

Cook's Notes:

Quick Kung Pao Sauce
makes about 1 1/2 cups
whisk

Add this sauce to any veggie stir-fry, just before serving, allowing a minute or two for the sauce to thicken as it heats. You could also make a larger batch, heat it in a saucepan, and pour it over a rice or noodle bowl. Top with chopped peanuts and red pepper flakes for even more of that kung pao "pow."

Ingredients
1 T arrowroot
1/2 cup cold water
1 T fresh grated ginger
1 T fresh minced garlic
1/4 cup tahini
3 T tamari - or to taste
3 T maple syrup
1 T umeboshi plum paste (optional)
1 T Sriracha sauce
1 T white vinegar

Instructions
Place the arrowroot in a medium sized bowl, and gradually whisk in the water until well blended, with no lumps. Add remaining ingredients and whisk until blended. Heat as directed above, either in a saucepan, or tossed right into a stir-fry. The sauce thickens as it heats.

Cook's Notes:

Easy Orange Sauce
makes about 1 cup
whisk

This sauce is particularly good with steamed or stir-fried vegetables. Consider broccoli, cauliflower, carrots, eggplant, onions, snap peas, and any others you love. It's also good over a rice bowl or any Asian-style noodle dish.

Ingredients
1/2 cup orange juice
1/4 cup tamari
2 T maple syrup
1 T Sriracha sauce
1 T arrowroot

Instructions
Whisk all ingredients together. Pour over stir-fried vegetables, just before they're done. Continue cooking until the sauce thickens and the vegetables are tender-crisp.

Variation
Make a double batch of this sauce and heat it gently in a saucepan. Pour over your finished dish at serving time.

Cook's Notes:

Cheesy Miso Sauce
makes about 3 cups
whisk

I used to add a lot of things to my little ramen noodle packs. Extra vegetables and seasonings made it more of a meal. Back then, I'd also add cheese. It was actually quite wonderful, and this reminds me of those good old ramen days. It's a thin-ish sauce, kind of on the brothy side, which makes it really good in a noodle or rice bowl. You can also thicken it by adding a little extra arrowroot.

Ingredients
3 cups water
3 T nutritional yeast
1/2 tsp garlic powder
1/4 tsp red pepper flakes (or a dash of hot sauce)
1 T tamari
2-3 T miso (to taste)
1-2 T arrowroot, for desired thickness

Instructions
Place all ingredients in a saucepan, and whisk together over medium heat until steaming. Don't boil your miso. It kills the friendly enzymes in it. Add more arrowroot if needed.

Cook's Notes:

Oil Free Basil Pesto
makes about 2 cups
food processor

When Rick and I had our pizza shop in Seattle, we went through mountains of fresh basil each week. The smell is heavenly, and always makes me feel happy. In this pesto, I use whole olives rather than olive oil, for a whole-food alternative that's every bit as rich and delicious as traditional pesto. Feel free to use oil if you like. I also replaced expensive pine nuts with walnuts.

Use pesto as a spread on bread or sandwiches, as a pizza sauce or topping, or as a pasta sauce. It's best to make only as much as you'll use right away.

Ingredients
2 cloves garlic
about 4 cups fresh basil leaves and tender stems
1 (6 oz) can pitted black olives
1/4 cup nutritional yeast
1/2 tsp salt
juice of 1/2 lemon (about 2 T)
1/2 cup walnut pieces
water to thin if necessary

Instructions
Place the garlic in the food processor first, and chop it for a few seconds all by itself.
Add half the basil, the olives, nutritional yeast, salt, and lemon juice.
Pulse to blend a little at a time, adding the remaining basil as you go.
Add the walnuts last and pulse a few more times. Don't over-blend pesto or it will go from vibrant green to an unappetizing khaki color.

Cook's Notes:

Creamy Glam Sauce
makes about 5 cups
blender or food processor

This elegant sauce is similar to clam sauce, thanks to the chewy mushrooms. It can transform ordinary pasta into an elegant dish worthy of serving to company. It also works well as a "gravy" over mashed potatoes, rice, or even biscuits. Try it on pizza, or simply set a warm bowlful on the table with chunks of crusty bread for dipping.

Ingredients
1 cup raw cashews, soaked 20 minutes or more
1/4 cup nutritional yeast
1 1/2 cups unsweetened plant-based milk
8 oz crimini mushrooms, cut into half inch pieces
4 oz fresh oyster mushrooms, cut into half inch pieces
1 oz dry shitake mushrooms, soaked 30 minutes in water, cut into half inch pieces
3 large cloves garlic, chopped
1/4 cup white wine
1/2 cup sun-dried tomatoes (softened if dry), chopped
1 cup fancy pitted olives of your choice, coarsely chopped (I picked an assortment from the olive bar at my local market)
1 cup chopped fresh basil
1/2 lemon, juiced (about 1-2 T)
salt and black pepper to taste

Instructions
Drain and rinse the soaked cashews, and place them in a blender or food processor with the nutritional yeast and milk. Blend until very smooth.
Sauté the mushrooms and garlic in the wine for about 5 minutes, over medium-high heat, until they start to dry out. Do not add extra liquid.

(cont.)

Reduce heat to medium, and pour in the blended cashew sauce. Add sun-dried tomatoes, olives, and basil, and cook for about 5 minutes, stirring often, and adding more milk, wine, or water if it gets too thick.

Season with salt and pepper to taste, and squeeze in the lemon juice just before serving. Garnish with a sprig of fresh basil, and maybe a little sprinkle of nutritional yeast and fresh ground black pepper.

Cook's Notes:

Mushroom-Cashew Gravy
makes about 4 cups
blender or food processor

Who doesn't love gravy? It's good on practically everything, and it's super easy to make. I've served this to some of my toughest-to-please friends, and they've all loved it.

Ingredients
1/2 yellow onion, chopped
3-4 cloves garlic, chopped
2 cups crimini mushrooms, chopped
1/4 cup raw cashews, soaked 20 minutes
1/4 cup nutritional yeast
1 tsp dry thyme
1 tsp dry basil
1/2 cup white wine
1 cup water
2-4 T tamari
salt and pepper to taste

Instructions
Sauté the onion, garlic, and mushrooms in a little water (or oil), over medium heat, until the onions are soft and transparent. Place the cashews in a blender, and carefully add the mushroom mixture. Add the nutritional yeast, herbs, wine, water, and tamari. Blend on high speed for about one minute, or until it's very smooth. Pour the gravy back into the saucepan, and warm over low heat. Add a little water if it's too thick, or a tablespoon of arrowroot mixed with cold water if it needs to thicken. Season with salt and pepper to taste.

Cook's Notes:

Heavenly Hollandaise
makes about 2 1/2 cups
blender or food processor

This sauce is so good on so many things. It has much less fat than traditional hollandaise, and zero cholesterol. Drizzle it over asparagus, broccoli, or any other vegetable you like, pour it on tofu scrambles and breakfast potatoes, and enjoy it with simple rice or noodle dishes. If you want to get fancy, make a Veggie Benny with English muffins, fried tofu, mushrooms, or eggplant, and sundried tomatoes, topped with hollandaise and a sprinkle of smoked paprika.

Ingredients
8 oz. (1/2 block) silken tofu
1/4 cup raw cashews, soaked 20 minutes
1/4 cup raw pine nuts, soaked with the cashews
1/4 cup nutritional yeast
1 tsp salt (or to taste)
1/8 tsp cayenne
1/4 tsp turmeric
1/8 tsp garlic powder
1/4 tsp dry Herbs de Provence or basil
1/4 cup lemon juice
1/2 cup water

Instructions
Place all ingredients in a blender or food processor, and blend until very smooth. Warm over low heat in a saucepan. (If you have a Vitamix, you can use boiling water and skip the saucepan.)

Cook's Notes:

Salad Dressings

I'm a firm believer in eating your greens. I generally fill half my plate with greens of some kind, cooked or raw, and the rest with whatever else I'm having, topped with a tasty sauce, of course. Salad is another easy way to fit greens into your meals, and certainly a salad can be a meal in itself. To pack in even more greens, chop them up rather than leaving them big and fluffy. You'll fit a lot more green goodness into the available space, and into you.

Salad dressings are nothing more than sauces for salads! They're easy to make, taste much better than store bought dressings, and they keep well for a week or more in the refrigerator. Eat them up, make more, repeat.

Basic Vinaigrette
makes about 1 cup
jar or whisk

This is as easy as it gets. So easy, it's barely a recipe!
The basic formula to follow is one part vinegar to three parts
oil.

Ingredients
1/4 cup balsamic vinegar
3/4 cup olive oil
salt and pepper to taste

Instructions
Place all ingredients in a jar. Close the lid tightly, and shake to
mix.

Variations
Use any kind of oils and vinegars you like. This is fun to
experiment with. Add dry or fresh herbs and spices, such as
basil, oregano, thyme, garlic powder, onion powder, chili
powder, cumin, curry powder, or dry mustard. For an Asian-
inspired dressing, substitute one part of the oil with toasted
sesame oil, and replace the vinegar with tamari or soy sauce.
Make lighter dressings by substituting fruit juice (orange and
grapefruit are nice) for some of the oil.

Cook's Notes:

Kim's Favorite Dressing
makes about 2 cups
blender

This dressing uses no oil at all. The nuts give it a nice whole food richness and a little healthy fat. A good Dijon mustard makes all the difference.

Ingredients
1/2 cup nutritional yeast
1/4 cup walnuts (or other raw nuts)
1/2 tsp garlic powder
1/2 tsp salt
black pepper to taste
1 tsp red pepper flakes
2 T tamari
2 T Dijon mustard
1/4 cup apple cider vinegar (or other vinegar)
juice of 1 lemon (about 3 T)
1 T maple syrup
1 cup water
1/2 - 1 cup fresh basil (optional)

Instructions
Place all ingredients into the blender, and buzz it up on high speed until well blended. This keeps at least a week in the refrigerator, and probably quite a bit longer. I always use it up before the week is out.

Cook's Notes:

Cheesy Basil Dressing
makes about 3 cups
blender or food processor

This is a thick, creamy, cheesy dressing that's reminiscent of the good old-fashioned blue cheese dressings of my early years. My husband loves it. I do too, and I like to mix it on my salad about half and half with *Kim's Favorite* (previous).

Ingredients
1 cup raw cashews, soaked 20 minutes
1/2 - 1 cup fresh basil leaves
1/2 cup nutritional yeast
1 tsp truffle salt (or regular salt)
1 tsp garlic powder
1 T Dijon mustard
1/4 cup apple cider vinegar (or balsamic or wine vinegar)
juice of 1/2 lemon (1-2 T)
1 cup water

Instructions
Place everything in a blender, and blend on high speed until smooth.

Cook's Notes:

Cashew Caesar Dressing
makes about 2 cups
blender or food processor

This is great on any kind of salad, but lends itself particularly well to a big bowl of romaine with anything else you like to toss in. Keep it traditional, with croutons and an extra squeeze of lemon, or take it in a southwest direction (see Variations below).

Ingredients
1 cup raw cashews, soaked in water for 20 minutes or more
2-3 cloves fresh garlic
1/4 cup nutritional yeast
1 tsp salt
1/4 cup olive oil
juice of 1 lemon (about 3 T)
1 cup water
1/2 tsp kelp granules (optional)
black pepper and extra salt to taste

Instructions
Drain and rinse the soaked cashews, place all ingredients in a blender or food processor, and blend on high speed until smooth. Add more water if necessary, for the right consistency.

Variation
Add fresh or dried herbs, such as basil, oregano, or thyme.
Add 1 tsp chipotle powder for a southwest dressing similar to one served at the Grand Canyon. Layer chopped romaine with black beans, corn, olives, red bell pepper, and avocado, and top with tortilla chips instead of croutons.

Cook's Notes:

Avocado-Orange Dressing
makes about 2 cups
blender

This oil-free dressing gets its healthy fat and satisfying richness from the avocado. It's good on just about any style of salad.

Ingredients
1 cup orange juice
juice of 1/2 lime (about 1 T)
1/4 cup Dijon mustard
1/2 cup apple cider vinegar
2 cloves garlic
1 T maple syrup
1 T ground flaxseed
1 avocado
1-3 tsp chile powder (or to taste)
1/8 tsp chipotle powder (or to taste)

Instructions
Place all ingredients in the blender, and blend on high speed until smooth. Adjust seasonings. The flaxseed will thicken the dressing after about 5 minutes.

Cook's Notes:

Spicy Greek Dressing
makes about 1 1/2 cups
blender or food processor

I think a great Greek Salad should be about half romaine or other greens, and half "stuff." The stuff is tomatoes, cucumbers, red onions, artichoke hearts, kalamata olives, pepperoncini, and tofu feta (bonus recipe follows). Not traditional, but delicious, is a sprinkle of roasted, salted sunflower seeds on top of everything.

Ingredients
1 cup raw cashews, soaked 20 minutes or longer
1-2 T fresh oregano
2 T nutritional yeast
1/2 tsp salt (or to taste)
1/2 cup juice from a jar of pepperoncini

Instructions
Place all ingredients in a blender or food processor. Blend on high speed until smooth and creamy.

Cook's Notes:

Tofu Feta

1 package extra firm tofu
2 cups water
juice of 2 lemons, (about 1/4 cup)
1 T salt
1 T dry basil
1 T dry oregano
2 T nutritional yeast

Press the tofu to remove most of the water. If you don't have a tofu press, wrap the whole block of tofu in a clean dishtowel, place it on a plate, and put a heavy weight on top of it for 15 minutes or so. I use my big cast iron frying pan as a weight.
Cut the pressed tofu into small cubes.
Place everything *but* the tofu in a saucepan, and bring it to a boil.
Add the tofu cubes, turn the heat down to med-low, and simmer gently for about 30 minutes.
Chill the tofu and liquid in the refrigerator for 8 hours or more - the longer the better. But if you're in a rush, it will still taste good with a shorter soak time.

Cook's Notes:

Simple Meals to Put Under Your Sauces

As I mentioned in the introduction, most people rely on just a handful of familiar recipes they can easily make and serve over and over again. We're creatures of habit, we like what we like, and we have less time than ever to make a lot of fuss over what's for dinner.

Plant based kitchens are often the same in that respect. I actually recommend learning to make a few simple dishes that you can easily repeat, but in endlessly different ways. If you've been eating this way for a while, you probably have a few favorites of your own. If not, try some of the following.

And by all means, even if you're not 100% plant-based yet, use the sauces in this book on your non-vegan dishes too. It's OK!

Grain Bowls

Sometimes called Buddha Bowls, these might be the easiest and most versatile of all plant-based meals. You need three key elements: a cooked whole grain, such as brown rice, quinoa, wild rice, farro, barley, millet, or whole wheat couscous, cooked vegetables, such as broccoli, carrots, onions, leafy greens, squash of any kind, eggplant, green beans, peas, corn, cabbage, etcetera, and a sauce that suits the combination you've chosen. Many of the sauces in this book are terrific with rice bowls. I particularly like Buddha Belly Sauce or Easy Orange Sauce for these, but also consider Thai Green Curry, Red or Green Chile, Cheese Sauce, and even Hollandaise.

Cook your grain first. While it's doing its thing, prep and cook your vegetables. Steaming, stir-frying, and oven roasting are all easy methods. Next make your sauce and keep it warm on the stove while everything else finishes cooking. Make extra everything so you'll get more than one meal out of your efforts. (cont.)

Assemble your bowl by placing the cooked grain in the bottom, topping it with vegetables, and finally ladling on the sauce. Garnish with sliced avocados, nuts or seeds, shredded raw vegetables, or hot sauce.

Variation: Use noodles, polenta, or mashed potatoes instead of cooked grain.

Cook's Notes:

Burritos and Wraps

Tortillas are pretty amazing. Fill one with beans, vegetables, greens, and vegan cheese, fold in the ends, roll it up, and you have a meal. Add Cheese Sauce or Red or Green Chile, and you have a feast.

Wraps are the same thing by a different name. How about stuffing your tortilla with cooked brown rice, steamed asparagus, sundried tomatoes, and spinach, and topping it with Hollandaise?
Or maybe a tofu-potato scramble filling with chopped kale or cabbage and a nice pool of Mushroom-Cashew Gravy?

Tortillas also shape shift into tacos (don't forget about corn tortillas), quesadillas (melt some vegan cheese on a tortilla in a frying pan, add vegetables, fold it in half, and serve with small bowls of your favorite sauces for dipping), and even pizza (layer 2 flour tortillas with vegan cheese in between, top with Basil Pesto or Cheese Sauce and your favorite veggies, and bake for a few minutes until it's hot and the edges are crispy.)

Cook's Notes:

Stir-Fries

Cooking vegetables in a large frying pan or wok in a little hot oil is fast and easy, and leaves room for limitless variety. I made a version of this several times a week when we first went vegan. I like a large skillet with a lid, since there's no room in my kitchen to store a wok. Choose a pan with plenty of room for stirring, and with a tight fitting lid.

Experiment with different combinations of vegetables and sauces, and maybe throw in some cooked rice or quinoa for a veg-heavy fried rice. Add cubed tofu, tempeh, or vegan "meat" for added texture and protein.

Good sauces for stir-fries include Kung Pao, Peanut Sauce, Green Curry, and Easy Orange Sauce.

To make a stir-fry, chop all your vegetables before you start cooking. It's a fast frying process and you'll need to stay with the pan.
Heat the pan first on medium-high to high heat, depending on your stove.
Once the pan is hot, add 2-3 tablespoons of oil. I like coconut oil for this because it can take the heat. (see the Oils section)
Add your chopped vegetables according to the time they'll take to cook. Harder vegetables will go in first. Stir them constantly for 2-3 minutes before adding softer vegetables.

One of my favorite combinations is onion, celery, and carrots, followed by brown rice, red bell pepper, and thinly sliced cabbage, then chopped kale, and finally broccoli.
Stir in each addition for 1-2 minutes.
When the broccoli turns bright green, add 2-3 tablespoons of water, and a splash of tamari to the pan, cover with a lid, and turn off the heat.
Let it sit for five minutes. The steam will finish cooking the broccoli.
Uncover and either stir in a sauce, or serve it on the side.

Cook's Notes:

Scrambles

Not just for breakfast, a hearty, filling scramble is commonly made with extra firm, cubed or crumbled tofu. Also consider tempeh, potatoes, grains, and even more exotic ingredients like sweet potatoes or jackfruit (get canned young jackfruit in water at Asian groceries).

Add vegetables, top with your choice of sauce, and you have a quick meal that can be served straight from the pan, or used as a filling for wraps, or in casseroles.

Depending on what goes into your scramble, just about any sauce in the book with be delicious with it. I particularly like Hollandaise, Cheese Sauce, Red or Green Chile, and Mole.

Scrambles are great when cooked with a little oil, but they can also be made in a non-stick pan with no oil at all.

To make a basic scramble, start with chopped onions, and maybe some garlic or celery in a hot pan with a little oil or water.
Once the onions are soft, toss in the tofu or other base listed above.
Cook that for about 3-5 minutes before adding vegetables, beans, nuts, seeds, herbs and spices.
Wilt in a big handful or more of chopped greens just before serving.

Cook's Notes:

Layered Casseroles

Just about anything can be layered in a casserole dish and baked. I love casseroles because once they're in the oven, I can wander off and do other things for 30 minutes to an hour while the baking goes on without me.

When making a casserole, you'll basically need three things – something to create the layers, something to put between the layers, and a sauce. Lots of sauce! Get creative with your casseroles. It's pretty hard to mess them up.

Some of my favorite combinations:

Cooked pasta, such as elbow macaroni or bow ties, pinto or black beans, diced green chiles, corn, tomatoes, and Cheese Sauce makes a wonderful winter comfort food. Try spicing it up with chili powder, or substituting corn tortillas for the pasta.

A baked dish of mashed potatoes, sautéed mushrooms and onions, carrots and green beans, topped with Mushroom-Cashew Gravy tastes like Thanksgiving any time of year, especially when you serve it with cranberries.

Layered enchiladas are much easier to make than rolled ones. Cut flour or corn tortillas in half so the straight sides fit to the edges of the baking pan. Layer them with any combination of things you like, such as spinach, mushrooms, beans, black olives, corn, and crumbled extra firm tofu, and ladle on some Red or Green Chile between the layers as well as on top.

Cook's Notes:

Salad Bar

I've noticed that we eat a lot more big salads if we don't have to make the whole thing every time. It's easy to prep several meals worth of vegetables and toppings, and store them in bowls or bags in the fridge so you can have an almost instant salad any time you want it.

Start with greens of any kind, including different lettuces, kale, spinach, and those wonderful triple-washed blends that are so super convenient.

Chop up crunchy veggies like carrots, celery, cabbage, radishes, jicama, and green onions.

Open and drain a can of any kind of beans. I like garbanzo, kidney, pinto, and black beans on salads.

Olives are nice in a salad, and so is corn. We also love pickles, pepperoncini, leftover cooked grains, pumpkin seeds or sunflower seeds, chopped nuts, and raisins.

Softer things like tomatoes and avocados are best chopped-to-order, but that's no big deal when most everything else is ready to go. Keep one or two of your favorite dressings on hand, and salad will soon become one of the easiest, most versatile meals to put together in a hurry.

Cook's Notes:

That's it! Thanks for reading, and cooking,
and feeding the best food you can to the people you love,
including your own sweet self.
Enjoy!
xo Kim

Made in the USA
Columbia, SC
20 June 2020